TOP TEN
FASTEST

Ruth Owen

A cheetah

CLASH

by

WISE WALRUS

ISBN: 978 1 84898 206 2

Copyright © *TickTock* Entertainment Ltd. 2010
First published in Great Britain in 2010 by *TickTock*,
The Pantiles Chambers, 85 High Street, Tunbridge Wells, Kent, TN1 1XP

Printed in China
3 5 7 9 10 8 6 4 2

Picture credits (t=top; b=bottom; c=centre; l=left; r=right; OFC=outside front cover):
Image courtesy of the Australian National Maritime Museum: Spirit of Australia is part of the museum's collection: 16–17,
29cl. Bloodhound SSC: 7. iStock: 1, 12–13, 24-25, 26t, 26b, 28bl, 29tl. NASA/courtesy of nasaimages.com: 18–19, 29br.
Emily Nathan/Getty Images: 23b. Shutterstock: 4, 5r, 14–15, 22, 23t, 27, 28tl, 28tr, 31. Skyscan Photolibrary/Alamy: 6,
29bl. Courtesy of SSC: 4–5bc, 8–9, 29tr. Keren Su/Corbis: 20–21, 29cr. Suzuki GB Plc: OFC, 2, 10–11, 28br.
© 2008 QWSR Ltd./Spline Design: 17t.

Thank you to Lorraine Petersen and the members of nasen

Every effort has been made to trace copyright holders, and we apologize in advance for any omissions.
We would be pleased to insert the appropriate acknowledgements in any subsequent edition of this publication.

NOTE TO READERS
The website addresses are correct at the time of publishing. However, due to the ever-changing
nature of the internet, websites and content may change. Some websites can contain links that
are unsuitable for children. The publisher is not responsible for changes in content or website
addresses. We advise that internet searches should be supervised by an adult.

The 2008 *Suzuki Hayabusa*

CONTENTS

INTRODUCTION

This book is all about the world's fastest things.

From **FAST** machines…

…to **FAST** birds…

…to **FAST** cars, planes and motorbikes.

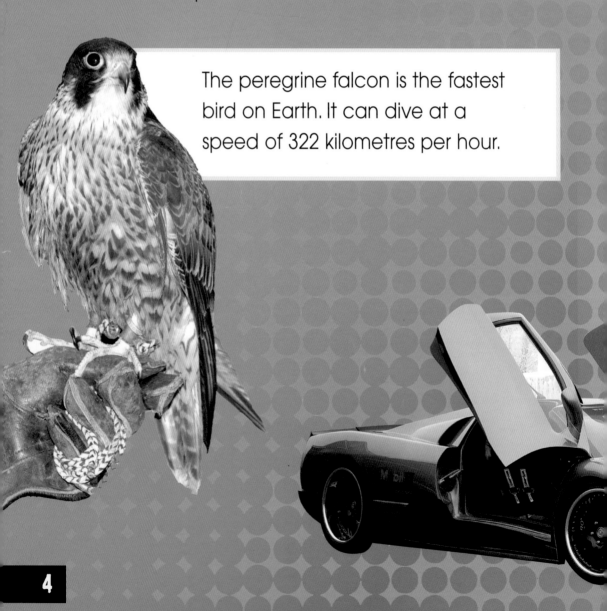

The peregrine falcon is the fastest bird on Earth. It can dive at a speed of 322 kilometres per hour.

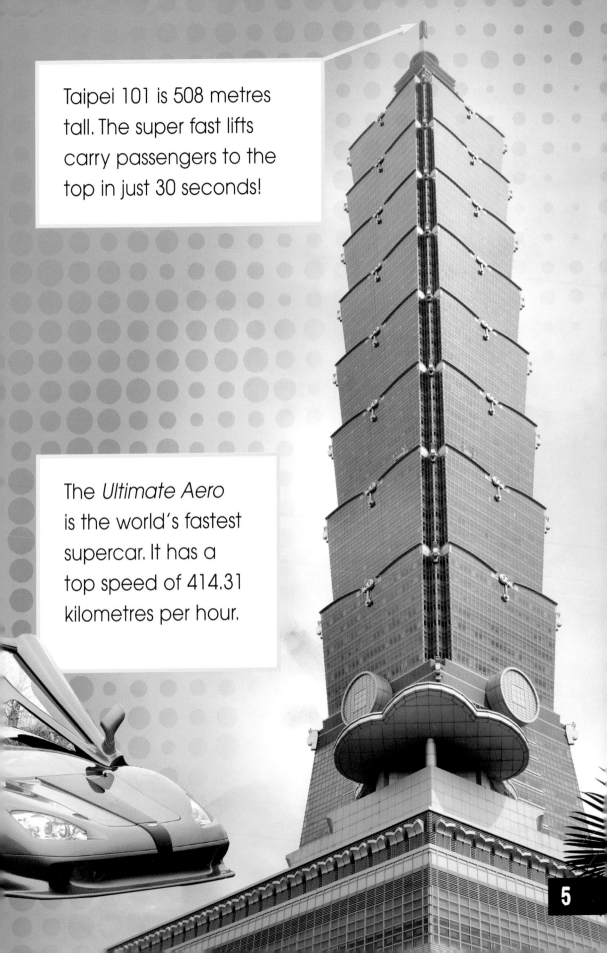

Taipei 101 is 508 metres tall. The super fast lifts carry passengers to the top in just 30 seconds!

The *Ultimate Aero* is the world's fastest supercar. It has a top speed of 414.31 kilometres per hour.

WORLD LAND SPEED RECORD

For over 100 years people have tried to travel the fastest on land.

The world land speed record is held by *Thrust SSC*. SSC stands for SuperSonic Car.

In 1997, *Thrust* went supersonic – faster than the speed of sound. It reached 1,227.985 kilometres per hour!

Thrust SSC

A team of engineers are planning a new record. They are building *Bloodhound SSC*.

Bloodhound SSC will be powered by a jet engine and rockets.

Bloodhound SSC

Richard Noble is the project director.

Andy Green will drive the car.

In 2011, *Bloodhound SSC* will try to go faster than 1,600 kilometres per hour.

FASTEST CAR

The *Ultimate Aero* is the world's fastest production car. This means it is a car that is produced for use on normal roads.

The *Ultimate Aero* is in the Guinness Book of World Records. The car made two test runs in front of testers from Guinness.

It reached 414.31 kilometres per hour on its first test run and 410.24 kilometres per hour on its second.

The average of the two speeds was used as the record-breaking speed of 412.28 kilometres per hour.

Ultimate Aero specs
- Made by Shelby Supercars in America
- Top speed: 414.31 kilometres per hour
- 0 to 97 kilometres per hour in 2.78 seconds

FASTEST MOTORBIKE

The world's fastest, most powerful motorbike is the *2008 Suzuki Hayabusa*.

It has a 1340 cc engine. It can reach speeds of 300 kilometres per hour. The bike can go faster than this, but for safety reasons its speed is restricted.

2008 Suzuki Hayabusa

FASTEST BIRD

The peregrine falcon is the fastest bird in a dive on Earth. It can dive on prey at more than 322 kilometres per hour.

The falcon gives its name to the fastest motorbike. The word "Hayabus" is Japanese for peregrine falcon.

Peregrine falcons mainly eat medium-sized birds. They also hunt for small mammals, reptiles and even insects.

The male and female look very similar but the female is bigger than the male.

Peregrine falcon

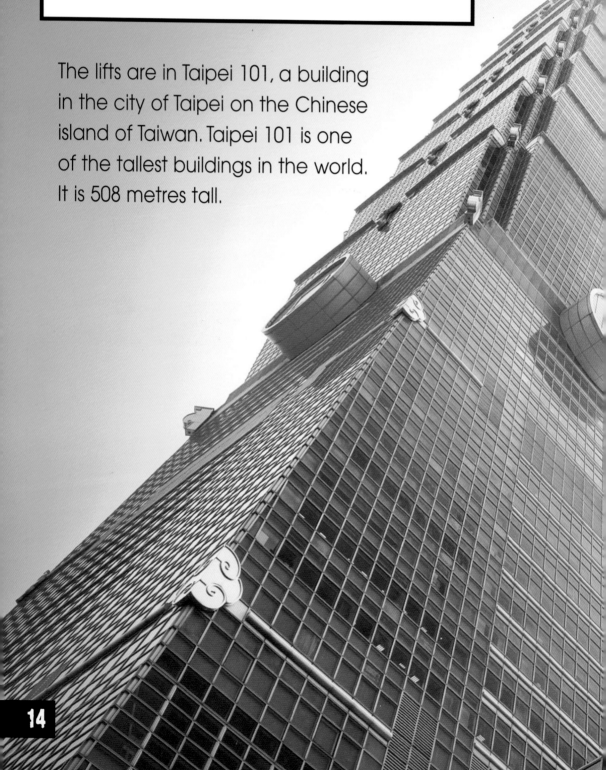

FASTEST LIFT

The world's fastest lifts travel upwards at 17 metres per second.

The lifts are in Taipei 101, a building in the city of Taipei on the Chinese island of Taiwan. Taipei 101 is one of the tallest buildings in the world. It is 508 metres tall.

The lifts are fitted with a special pressure system. This system stops the ears of passengers from popping!

WATER SPEED RECORD

For nearly 100 years people have tried to be the fastest on water.

The world water speed record is 511.11 kilometres per hour.

This record was set in 1978 by an Australian named Ken Warby. The boat was called *Spirit of Australia*.

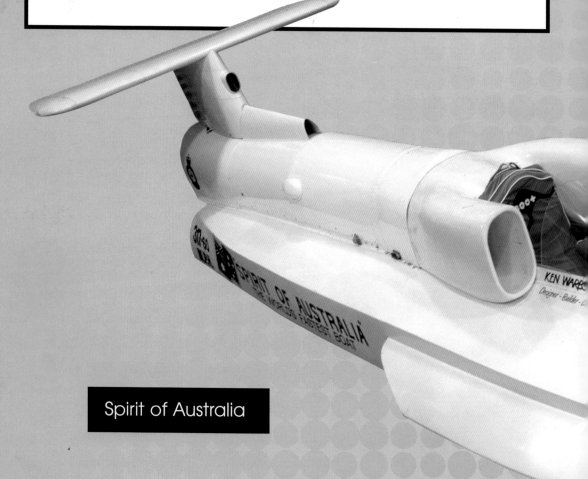

Spirit of Australia

Quicksilver

A team of British engineers want to break
this record. They are building a boat named
Quicksilver. It will be driven by Nigel Macknight.

Quicksilver will try to break the water speed
record in 2012.

FASTEST AIRCRAFT

The *X-43A* is the fastest jet-powered aircraft. It is an experimental aircraft and was built by scientists at NASA.

The *X-43A*'s engine uses air in a special way. Scientists believe this will allow planes to fly at thousands of kilometres per hour.

It will also allow rockets to go into space carrying less fuel and more cargo.

X-43A

The *X-43A* does not have a pilot. It takes off on a *B-52B* plane. A booster rocket launches the *X-43A*. Then the *X-43A*'s engine takes over!

In 2004, the *X-43A* reached a speed of nearly 11,260 kilometres per hour.

FASTEST TRAIN

The fastest type of train in the world is the Maglev train. Its name stands for "magnetic levitation".

Maglev train

Magnets are used to lift the train above a special track. Then magnets are used to guide and move the train.

The world's only commercial Maglev railway is in China. The Shanghai Transrapid line is 30 kilometres long.

The fastest speed recorded for a Maglev train was 581 kilometres per hour. This was during a test run in Japan.

FASTEST GROWING PLANT

Bamboo is a woody, evergreen type of grass. It is the fastest growing plant in the world.

There are around 1,000 different types of bamboo. Some types can grow up to one metre in a single day!

Bamboo is very strong. It can be used as a building material.

A temple in Indonesia being built from bamboo

Bamboo can be used to make all sorts of things including clothes and cutlery.

FASTEST MAMMAL

The world's fastest mammal is the cheetah. Over a short distance a cheetah can run at 113 kilometres per hour.

Every part of a cheetah's body is designed for speed:
- Large nostrils and lungs to take in more air
- A long, streamlined body and thin bones
- Special paw pads and claws to help push off from the ground
- A spine which works as a spring for the powerful back legs

ANIMAL SPEED FREAKS

The fastest water mammals are orcas and Dall porpoises. They can swim at up to 56 kilometres per hour.

Orca

Dall porpoise

Ostriches are the fastest birds on land.
They can run at 72 kilometres per hour.

Ostrich

TOP TEN FASTEST

Some of the fastest things on Earth were created by nature.

Others were built by humans.

They are all amazing record-breakers.

10

Fastest growing plant:

Bamboo, grows up to one metre per day

9

Fastest lift:

Taipei 101, 17 metres per second

8

Fastest mammal:

Cheetah, 113 kilometres per hour

7

Fastest motorbike:

2008 *Suzuki Hayabusa*, 300 kilometres per hour

6

Fastest bird:

Peregrine falcon,
322 kilometres per hour

5

Fastest production car:

Ultimate Aero,
414.31 kilometres per hour

4

Fastest boat:

Spirit of Australia,
511.11 kilometres per hour

3

Fastest train

Maglev train,
581 kilometres per hour

2

Fastest on land:

Thrust SSC,
1,227.985 kilometres per hour

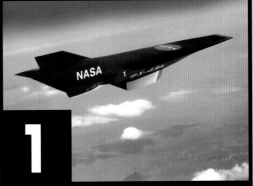

1

Fastest aircraft:

X-43A,
11,260 kilometres per hour

NEED TO KNOW WORDS

cargo Goods or equipment carried in a vehicle, such as a lorry, a plane or in a boat.

commercial Something that is done as a business with customers who pay.

evergreen A type of plant that has leaves all year around.

experimental Something that is part of an experiment, or something that is being tried out or tested.

Guinness World Records An organization that records and measures record-breaking things and events. The world records are then published in a book each year.

levitation When something rises and floats in the air.

mammal An animal with fur or hair that gives birth to a live baby and feeds it with milk from its own body. A mammal's body temperature stays the same no matter how hot or cold the air or water is around it.

NASA (National Aeronautics and Space Administration). NASA is an organization of the American government that runs the USA's space programme.

speed of sound Sound is a vibration. In air that vibration travels at about 1,225 kilometres per hour. It's about four times as fast in water.

supersonic Faster than the speed of sound.

SUPERSONIC AIRLINER

- *Concorde* was the world's only supersonic commercial airliner.

- It flew at around 2,170 kilometres per hour. That is almost twice the speed of sound.

Concorde

- A *Concorde* could fly from London to New York in around three hours 20 minutes. A *Boeing 747* takes more than seven hours to make the trip.

- Between 1976 and 2003, 2.5 million passengers travelled on *Concorde*.

- The fleet of *Concordes* is no longer flying. No other supersonic commercial airliner has replaced them.

FIND OUT MORE ONLINE...

http://www.bloodhoundssc.com/

http://www.shelbysupercars.com/car-specs.php

http://www.quicksilver-wsr.com/quicksilver

INDEX